PULLIN(

Zakariye is a poet, playwright and filmmaker from Birmingham. His short poetry film *Cages* was broadcast on BBC 4 and BBC iPlayer. Zakariye later went on to win the audience vote at the 2023 Roundhouse Poetry Slam final, cementing his place as a voice to watch. He is now a Roundhouse Resident Artist and a member of Birmingham Hippodrome Origins working on a brand new play, also titled *Cages*, that dives into the complexities of friendship, youth and navigating the challenges of growing up in the ends.

First published in 2025 by Little Betty, an imprint of Bad Betty Press
Cobden Place, Cobden Chambers, Nottingham NG1 2ED

badbettypress.com

PB ISBN: 978-1-913268-86-2
EPUB ISBN: 978-1-913268-87-9

A CIP record of this book is available from the British Library.

Book design by Amy Acre

Supported using public funding by ARTS COUNCIL ENGLAND
LOTTERY FUNDED

Pulling Faces

ZAKARIYE

For younger me, respectfully

LITTLE BETTY

CONTENTS

BAGGY DAD GENES

Wait.
How dare this man
wear dad's face?
Who taught him to sport
jack-up jeans and odd socks?

Wait.
He actually walks
with the same bop
hands behind his back
fingernails filled to the margin.

Someone ask him why he's
squinting when there's no sun.
Thought only our dad did that.
Except now he shakes awake
cigarettes the way dad does
        and offers me one. How'd he know
to offer me one? Swear this guy holds
trauma like he owes it a favour.

Swear he looks just like us.
Swear he's just like dad.

Except he is not him.
He is better.
He is here.

PULLING FACES

Make our wrinkles cross over like argyle.
Give us melasma, liver spots, hyperpigmentation.
Burst our faces with reminders of uncles taken
too soon and aunts that aren't here. Place your thumb
on our chin, take in every trace of skin. Dark parts
on creases. Large scars on elbows and arms
from treating concrete like carpet. Remember
the abandoned dirt green merc opposite mine?
How the door popped open, splashed silence
over front doors? We sat under your grandma's scowl
that day. Planned all possible escapes from her face.
We had every exit covered. Found a shortcut
on the corner of Cataracts. Before you reach Melasma,
you want to take a left by Liver Spots and there you'll find it
younger you   hidden amongst skin conditions.

NIGEL

Nigel, the block's stray cat jumps with wide eyes
        skin so dark it's purple.
Generational whispers would sing to my mother
        curse the devil when you see black.
She was on job g checking black cats and staring down
        abrasive crows.
Even the more melanated pigeons weren't
        safe from getting sharked.
Her voice grew hoarse with my name until
        it itched like a tattoo on her palate.
When she finally saw me, her eyes turned gloomy
        like the Great Dane on my bed.
All her superstitions came barrelling. Do not:
        cut your nails at night,
scratch your right palm, step over a sleeping person,
        stand next to trees after dark.
When my eyes opened, all was silent. Her hand rested on
        the dog, wet from the rain.
No words.   Later, I saw her
        feeding Nigel on our doorstep.

On the kitchen table;
a half-assembled bird house.

THOBE IN A TOTE BAG

A good human from the scene will see
you on a Friday walking to mosque
dripped out in your favourite thobe.
They will ask you about your clothes.
Yeah man it's a Friday
so I'm usually dressed like this for prayer.
You will hope they misheard you
when they mention
how they do quick shop runs
in their PJs too.

TELL ME HOW YOUR UNCLE CALLS YOU UNCLE

My uncle misses two fingers
and as kids we would speculate

I heard it was a Rottweiler
        Nah I heard he tried catching a bullet
                What?? I heard he was born like that

One time, I mustered the courage to ask.
        Uncle?
Hmm.
        How'd you get like that?
Like what.
        That.

He held up the nothingness.
Speechless, I assembled the smallest of nods.

Time is a watery friend. Go for a drive in the night.
Turn the radio up loud. Take in your friend's face.
Pull the window down and throw your hand against the air.

I gulped the emptiness trapped in my throat.
        Is that how it happened?
How what happened.
        That.
Oh, this. No. No it was worse. Much worse.

I WOULD 8-2 BE YOU

Chat to a man

:with proper posture
protected by grandparent's prayers

:who can stretch a 20 note so long
you'd swear there's a zero missing

:who'd have your hands dance over
an open handshake and closed spud

:chatting about how to overcome
the killing of their kid's community centre

:whose life you couldn't live
without devouring his scabs

:who yams food on his ones
in public no earphones

:who juggles love with two left hands
and struggles treasuring tiny moments

that find their way there –
:that says *them way there*

about any hindrance
be it a bereavement

or the football score.

BIGGER BROTHER, BIGGER COUSIN

Yesterday they stole your clip-on tie
today they might make you grow up.

WHO ARE YOU TO SAY NO?

Bigger kids parade playgrounds
in search of faces to snatch.
WHO DO YOU KNOW? To rush you,
stuff you into the mud.

You sound like a puppy YOU GOT
you sound like a lost thing A BIGGER BROTHER
you make noise to make noise
you are perfect picking. BIGGER COUSIN?

THAT'S A NICE BAG Fenced in
Y'KNOW. swarmed by serpent faces.
Learn to become limbless.

I LIKE YOUR WATCH AS WELL.

Search for small snakes
hanging off of smaller necks.

WHERE'S IT FROM? Slowly
coil clip-on ties
into blazer pockets.

Do not look up.   WHERE YOU FROM?
Bigger kids will only look bigger.

WHO'S HERE FOR YOU?

PRAYER MAT IN A TOTE BAG

Someone you vaguely know
will walk in on you prostrating
in the cloakroom of a hefty venue.
They will half-whisper an apology and
shuffle away. Later that night you message them

Hey sorry I was praying when you walked in lol
I wasn't ignoring you on purpose

They will respond with how much
they *loooved* the pattern
on your yoga mat.

~~NO~~ BALL GAMES ALLOWED

Dead that sign / dead the neighbour as well / heard she got it off Amazon / it's defo not a council one / I already said bagsy not jumping over / everyone knows I jumped it last time / plus she knows my face now / trust me she's not home / her car's not in the drive / it has to be you bro / everyone's jumped it before / I beg / go on quickly / before she comes back / I'll give you a leg up / easy / nice one / kick it over first / yeah I got it / what / say that again / what do you mean you can't jump back over / okay relax man / let me think / do you see any flowers / yeah the ones in the pots / you see them yeah / yeah / dead them / dead / them / flip them over / stack them if you need to / stand on them quick and reach / are you even trying / reach man / wait / that's her car pulling in right now / stop making so much noise / I'm throwing over a bit of my coat / you got it yeah / on three pull as hard as you can / ready / … / one / … / two / … / three

PULL /

that's it bro / almost there / quick man / she's speedwalking over / phone to her ear / threats of the police / but don't watch that / I can see your hand / hold on / okay / deep breath / you ready / you sure / okay / dip / don't even look back / just sprint / alright push the bins out the way / squeeze through the gap / quick man / come help me push the bins back / make it look good / I say we go Viccy park / she won't find us there / she didn't see your face /

trust me she didn't / I would've clocked if she did / she's known my face for time / but she don't know where I live / yeah exactly it's not deep / calm down bro / you did bits / did you dash her flowers / oh swear / how'd you jump back over then / mad / fair play / if you saw the way I dashed her flowers / I didn't even think twice / they were gone / but you've always been like that / caring about stuff / nah I'm not judging you / I'm just saying / you're good enit / you're actually good.

THE HIM.

The two tallest figures at the departure gate
embrace, hold abandoned bones.

The older contains the younger's face.
The younger pockets this moment for later.

The older tosses and turns in his mind
when will you come up again?

Palms hollowing, carving room
to store a growing body,
malleable face, voice cracks,
five o'clock shadows.

Trade a return ticket for more time apart.
A renewed passport for missed phone calls.
From settling old scores to settling old and alone.

Tell him you'll be back in autumn.
That you'll miss the harvest,
the sun,

the hymn.

THE HER.

The two opposing figures at the arrival gate
come apart, release nourished souls.
Her eyelash rests on his cheek.
He'll see it in the mirror when she's gone.

Her answer sleeps sound in his heart
as soon as I can, promise.

Hands filling, losing ground
to laugh at jokes that don't land,
a stubborn face, noisy thoughts,
five o'clock shift ends.

Trade a bus pass for rushed pasts.
Inner city transport for after dinner night walks.
From settling old scores to settling old and alone.

Tell her you can't wait for spring.
That you'll miss the traffic,
the moon,

the hurt.

THE ULTIMATE TRAVEL GUIDE

Your old man takes us to all the houses he grew up in.
Has us run our hands across bullet holes in the walls.
Does dishes in a missing sink.
Leads us down a street.
Points at places with an umbrella he found.
His old school, the tuition centre, a care home.
Looks at us like we called his name.
            Holds for a second – hurries off.
Car parks turned to makeshift football grounds.
Bus shelters he got robbed at.

He prays in the rubble.
Makes dua amidst the dust.
Sends prayers upon the Prophet, whispers *peace be upon him*.
Lies on the floor so still the ground settles him in.
You place a duvet we can't see over his body.
Tuck it up to his beard, feet covered.
Your old man smiles in his sleep.

TASBIH IN A TOTE BAG

You will be doing dhikr on your walk back
from mosque, tasbih bending through fingers
when someone who means but rarely does well
asks about the *vintage necklace* in your hand.
It's not really a necklace; it's for counting prayers.

In answer to their questions, blood will weep
from your ears, pause at your shoulders
like giving advice, run down your arm
dye your tasbih in coloniser's colours.

Notice how they all have a variation of red and white.
The French, English, Danes, Italians, Dutch.
Hand over the *necklace*.

Give up the thobe stuffed in your tote.
Turn in the prayer mat with the *nice patterns.*

Waves carry people like you. Water takes you in.

I DID YOUR BIDDING

after Gboyega Odubanjo

learnt your language left my one behind turned up on time spoke when spoken to stayed silent for your minute sang your assembly songs sat cross-legged got my pen licence kept out of trouble passed your GCSEs went to your unis found one of your jobs pretended to enjoy it chipped away at my debt went through some dire talking stages met a girl with real skin invited strangers to our wedding saved for your downpayment called it quits after two years heard she was pregnant after two months tried to make it work talked to her father started therapy plunged into avoidant attachment bought her late-night crispy tofu stood in a hospital room for hours held our child like stale bread shook her father's hand took our new human home laid them in the cot we built dropped on the bed we bought superglued our limbs together realised her hair got stuck on my neck spent ages searching for scissors caught ourselves in the hallway mirror pulling the same face: bracing for impact.

ACKNOWLEDGEMENTS

Thank you Hooyo
Thank you Hooyo
Thank you Hooyo
Thank you Aabo.

Without you both there's nothing; with you both there's everything.

Thank you to my little sister for always humbling me.

Thank you to the rich Birmingham poetry scene. From my first open mic where my hands were shaking harder than my voice to the completion and existence of this pamphlet.

To Casey Bailey for your relentless jokes that never fail to contain the realest gems.

To Jasmine Gardosi for your undying passion and countless hours of generosity.

To Steven 'Polarbear' Camden who I'm still in absolute awe of despite all the time we've spent together catching trains and catching strays from primary school kids.

To Cecilia Knapp for all your words of wisdom and encouraging me to publish in my own time and not anyone else's.

To Kamil Mahmood whose first collection made poetry click in my mind and whose words of encouragement actually work, every conversation is gold.

To Nafeesa Hamid for your mastery in this craft, every performance pushes a boundary and unlocks something new in my brain.

To Aaisha Akhtar for your relentless work in pushing the arts and looking after artists (and getting me through uni).

To Bohdan Piasecki for your necessary good cop demeanour and constant warmth that helped me find my footing when I was starting out – we'll talk.

To Roger Robinson for your necessary bad cop demeanour and invaluable words that pushed me to view myself as an artist back when I couldn't see it.

To Yomi Ṣode for being the most serious unserious person in the poetry world – thank you for the much-needed talks.

To Deanna Rodger for being the kindest soul in the poetry world – thank you for the laughs and reality checks.

To every creative that I've had the privilege of calling a friend: THANK YOU. There are too many of you to name, which is a problem I'm very grateful to have. You're all wonderful inspiring human beings and lifesavers.

Thank you to the Bad Betty family for your trust in the way I arrange 26 letters. Amy Acre and Jake Wild Hall are absolute dons of the poetry world.

Thank you to Vanessa Kisuule for being the coolest and best editor. I've never namedropped anyone the way I've namedropped you.

And thank you to younger me for always PULLING FACES.

All praise be to God.

www.ingramcontent.com/pod-product-compliance
Ingram Content Group UK Ltd.
Pitfield, Milton Keynes, MK11 3LW, UK
UKHW011831081125
464835UK00006B/168

9 781913 268862